IRELAND

A Photographic Journey

PATRICK MAHÉ • PHILIP PLISSON ⚓

IRELAND

A Photographic Journey

BARNES
&NOBLE
BOOKS
NEW YORK

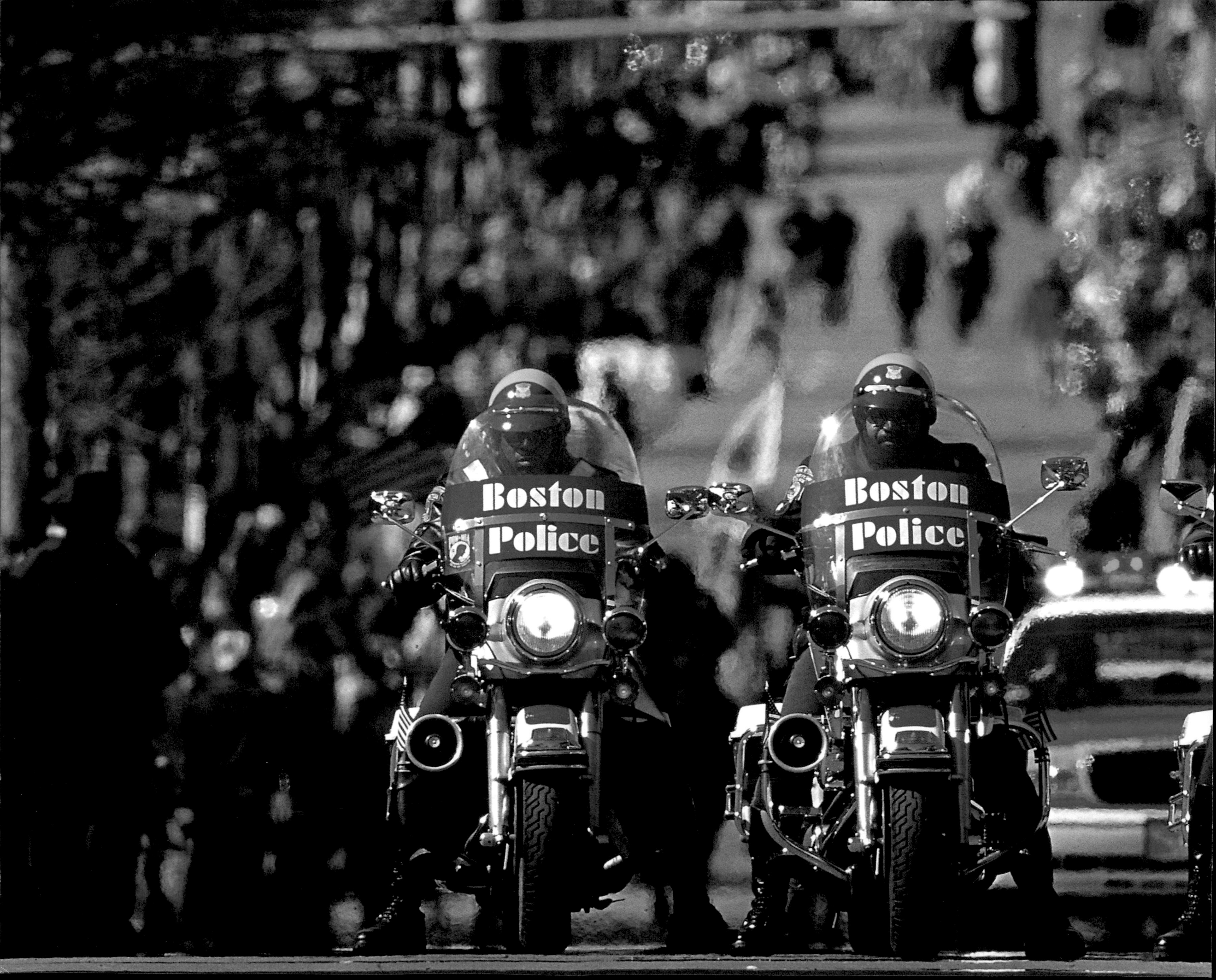
Boston
Police
Boston
Police

Ode to Saint Patrick

On this day, a bag piper proudly breathes life into his bagpipe. He's dressed in the plaid colors of his clan. (Only the Irish kilt is uniformly green). He wears a white rosette on his bonnet like those worn in the Battles of the Boyne (Ireland, 1690) and of Culloden (Scotland, 1746).

The 17th of March is Saint Patrick's Day. This day is celebrated around the world and "Around the Clock" just as Bill Haley sang in that old rock'n roll song of the 50's.

Dawn has already risen on the Aran Islands. They are the guardians of the entrance to the Bay of Galway, the gateway to Connemara. They shield Ireland's traditions. Gaelic is still the mother-tongue here just like it is in Skye, the winged island of the Hebrides in Scotland. Their waters are amongst the purest in Europe. Their flora is a botanist's paradise. Their archaeological sites make it a natural outdoor museum. Beyond the ocean, lies America…

It's still night over Cape Cod, south of Boston, the Irish capital of the New World. On the day of the parade, people will wear the *féile-beag*, a short and pleated kilt.

As for Australia, in Queensland, south of the Great Barrier Coral Reef, Mackay, Brisbane, and Sydney (New South Wales), twilight is embraced preparing for another green sleepless night.

Green, green, this world is green.

Everywhere, tradition is rekindled forming a universal Celtic bond. Participants in these festivities decorate their woolen and feathered bonnets with the white rosette, symbol of the Scottish and Irish Catholic dynasties crushed in the grinder of history.

On their hearts, they pin the green clover symbolizing the Holy Trinity and if, by chance, it has four leaves, it's a sign of good luck, a gift from the heavens.

Saint Patrick's Day is like Celtic New Year.

While Belfast, somber with its ghettos, prays to put an end to its Troubles, Dublin, the emancipated beauty, vivid and modern, glamorous and joyful, parades in full light. At the same time, their Celtic sisters Quimper and Saint-Malo (in Brittany, France), ring out in sea shanties on the coastline and under the ramparts.

Lorient also honors its pipers as it does at the peak of its summer festival. In the past, it was the sailing port for India and the dreams of Asia, the maritime route to spices and silk.

In Glasgow, Scottish cousins reel and rock around Celtic Park.

Celebrants don't parade any less proudly in New York, at the foot of Saint Patrick's Cathedral on Fifth Avenue. And while Chicago shows off, Boston sends all its parishes – even the Celtic basketball team - to the ritual procession.

And finally, Australia gallops ahead at full stride! At Broken Hill race track, jovial crowds bet on the majestic pace of thoroughbreds... with the symbolic blessing of the Holy Apostle.

March 17th is a public holiday on the Irish planet…A day of celebration for the little green men of the Celtic Diaspora.

They are brothers of the Scottish Highlanders, the loyal clans and the children of *Braveheart*.

The Bretons of the Armor Coast in Brittany are their cousins… Like those of Wales, of insular Cornwall, of the Isle of Mann, of Galicia and Asturia, Patrick is their hero of the day. For eternity.

From their varnished toes to their extravagant fluorescent wigs, they show him off on this day, flamboyantly mixing bad taste and emotional excess: "Kiss me, I'm Irish" proclaims their mass-produced tee-shirts.

Many red-headed women have thus spent their first night of love.

So, from Chicago on the banks of Lake Michigan, to the mouth of the Savannah, to the Liffey River, from the borders of the Irish Sea and up to the coral reefs of the South Pacific, the mythic Saint sees his flock transformed into drunken angels.

FOR PAGES 4-5

Today sixty million Americans are of Irish origin and refer to themselves as Irish-Americans.

70 million people of Irish origin, scattered by the winds of history (the defeat of James II by William of Orange on the Boyne, close to Drogheda, in Derry, and the Great Famine of 1848 – 700,000 dead) join the four million islanders in one collective festival.

From The Pogues to Sinead O'Connor (Ireland), to Dan Ar Braz (Brittany) whose music is in the Celtic tradition, from the pipe bands of Scotland and Nova Scotia, up to the Welsh choirs and harpists, the spirit of Saint Patrick flourishes…The green fever.

Thus, the elegant Irish *ceili*, pronounced kaylee, a ballet for tiny fairies and elves, attracts ecstatic crowds.

You'd think you were in *Riverdance*.

This show, discovered while it was being played as an interlude during the Eurovision Song Contest in 1994, has enchanted the world. It owes its success to its magical choreography. It brings us back to time immemorial, to the blacksmith's hound and Cuchulainn (the central character in a series of Celtic legends). This is the opening for the first tableau.

We are far, but not in spirit, from the *fest-noz Amoricain*. During the last two or three decades, the open-air festival has awakened all of Brittany, France, including Trégor and around the region of Vannes, the ramparts of Clisson, Guérande and the marches in the region of Nantes and the Duchess Anne.

While the sprites of *Riverdance* take off on violins in Dublin, Boston and Sydney, the Bretons of the Armor Coast stick to their roots. They dance arm in arm in joyous gavottes, stamping on wooden floors and dreaming under the stars. The *binious koz* or old biniou and the bombard (ancient Celtic instruments) keep the memory of a rural and sea-faring people intact.

The jig, an Irish folk dance, the reel, a Scottish folk dance, gavottes and the *laridé* from the Armor Coast all have the same history. The bombard, Breton oboe, gaïta, Galician bagpipe, *uileann pipe* (the Irish bagpipe) all underwent the same repression and are now going through a renaissance.

These instruments all played the music of simple shepherds.

Cromwell banned Celtic music in Ireland, four centuries ago.

Culloden sounded the last charge of the Scottish clans.

Castile stifled it, subjugating Asturias and Galicia in the name of an indivisible Spain.

Brittany battled against Jacobin uniformity.

Today, a common drive, a refreshing breath of solidarity, revives the same music across the seas.

Saint Patrick is the inspiration for this small miracle and the strong emotion it evokes. The holy holiday that bears his name overshadows those of his peers in Celtic sainthood – Saint Andrew, patron Saint of

The Galway, in Lorient, is the capital of Celtic music. It is here that the Irish community comes together traditionally to celebrate Saint Patrick's Day.

Scotland and Saint Yves, the patron of Brittany. Truly a fine destiny!

Patrick was born during the last decade of the fourth century, probably in Kilpatrick, Scotland, near Dumbarton. A Breton from Wales, he referred to himself as "Breton-Roman." His father bore the Roman name Calpurnius, perhaps by adoption. His mother's name was Conchessa. Little is known about his childhood. At fourteen, whilst still an adolescent he was kidnapped by pirates. Were they Scottish or Welsh? The legend remains a little vague but at their hands his head was cropped, he was dressed in a simple sheepskin and sold as a shepherd to a Northern Irish Druid from Antrim County. Later he would convert the son and the two daughters of the family…

Patrick was inhabited by visions and dreams. He took up God's cause. One night, a voice commanded him: "Return home. A ship awaits you." He was twenty years old.

Again it was a pirate ship. Answering what he believed to be a divine command, Patrick laid his destiny in the hands of the pirates. The ship landed in a miserably poor part of Wales. Patrick saved them from starvation, making a herd of wild boars appear by praying.

Not until the age of forty did Patrick finally prepare his return to Ireland. He provisioned a *curragh*, a small boat made from hide, for the journey. Today these same boats still sail between the isles of Aran. He crossed the sea alone.

He docked the boat at the gates of Tara, capital of Ard Ri, the supreme King. A pagan court flourished here, plentiful in Druids and

Green, green…a whole world of green. It rekindles in all the long guarded memory of the tradition of these people and binds them with the chain of universal loyalty. The more rebellious ones decorate their woolen or feathered bonnets with the white rosette emblems of those Scottish and Irish Catholic dynasties that have been crushed in the grinder of history.

Holy People. Patrick won them all over to his faith.

Saint Patrick made Ireland his Eden. He is present everywhere: In the north of Dublin and the vestiges of the sanctuary of Slane, where he lit the Easter. Fire to defy the Druids and the Holy Ones. In the county Mayo, where Croaigh Patrick mountain peaks at a height of 760 meters (2493 feet). In Donegal and the Isle of Lough Derg, known as the Red Lake.

It is here that Conan, son of Finn Mac Cool, the warrior and giant of Ireland, was said to have carelessly created a marine monster worthy of the Loch Ness legend in Scotland. With flair worthy of a modern Hollywood script, he let himself be devoured by the monster so that he could cut him up from the inside…There isn't really anything new about *Godzilla* or *Jurassic Park*!

In Ireland, such a legend demands the aura and presence of Saint Patrick. The second act in the story is completely consecrated to him. The monster was only hurt not slain; Patrick the Apostle dealt him the deathblow and the Lough Derg, reddened by the blood of the agonizing beast, has since the twelfth century become *Saint Patrick's Purgatory*. Today, the island is called Station Island and is marked with the stations of penance imposed on its pilgrims.

In this revered place, Patrick is represented alongside Saint Brigid, the patron saint of Ireland whose memorial is sculptured on an exterior wall of the Basilica. Also present are Saint Brendan and Saint Colomban. Here pilgrims spend their time praying and reciting "Our Fathers" and "Hail Marys," an infuriation to the fanatics of Northern Ireland's Reform Church of Ulster.

And nevertheless, it is here in this Northern Ireland, bruised and bloodied by four centuries of religious wars, that Saint Patrick lies.

Dawnpatrick takes pride in having the honor of watching over his remains. He died in Saul, on the peninsula near Lecale, where the tourist office invites visitors to follow "Saint Patrick's way." There are three walking tracks that follow the Saint's footsteps. You can see the presumed valley from where white buffaloes transported his body to the Anglican Church of Dawnpatrick.

Here, under a menhir, lies the pride of the reformed church of Ireland, whose beliefs contested the faithful of the "Papist" religion.

Fifteen centuries later, the effects are still evident. All over the world, there are parades in his name.

In Boston, on Atlantic Avenue which runs from Battery Wharf to Sargent's Wharf, marching pipe bands play their tunes resplendent in costumes of serpentine green.

In the crowd, there's a *Pêcheur d'Images* – also the name of Philip Plisson's trawler. And here begins the new travel log by Philip Plisson from Trinité in Brittany. His Trinité-sur-Mer. His book on Ireland could have started anywhere from Dublin to Belfast or Glasgow or from any Irish fief of Scotland or even Sydney…

It was on the 17th day of March under the universal pan Celtic sign that it began and it had, to be sure, the benediction of Saint Patrick.

Saint Patrick's Day is a little like a Celtic New Year. 70 million people of Irish origin, spread by the winds of history – the defeat of James II by William of Orange on the Boyne, in Derry, and the Great Famine of 1848 (700,000 dead) join the four million islanders in one collective festival.

PUB CULTURE IN DUBLIN

When Philip Plisson arrived in Ireland, his bag full of photos, he naturally followed in the Apostle's footsteps. Saint Patrick is everywhere on the Emerald Isle. Especially in a glass of *uisghe beatha*, that holy water called whiskey!

After his maritime tour of Scotland, it was only natural that *Pêcheur d'Images* (Philip Plisson's trawler) dock on the sister Island. He sailed close to the Stanraer Peninsula at the foot of the Eildan Hills.

It is there, in the fifth century, the same era of Saint Patrick, King Arthur came to take a look at his Celtic kingdom…

Ireland is part of this mythology. The Round Table and its Knights…these tales provide sustenance for novels of the Arthurian legend.

The Round Table turns in representation of cosmic power and influence. It symbolizes the wheel. It is also the symbol of the magic Celtic circle. With the shamrock, the clover and the harp, the Celtic cross is one of the symbols of Ireland.

Its four leaves symbolize the seasons and the cardinal points.
– To the East, Dublin is tender
– To the South, Cork is unruly
– To the West, Galway is harsh
– To the North, Belfast rebellious
Dublin is the first stop, the first haven. The Irish capital inspires life and youth but most of all a love of life.

The waters of the Liffey River are black and Dublin is named after it: *Dubb-linn* in Gaelic means black water. It is said to be as black as Guinness.

Beer belongs to Ireland. It is Ireland's trademark for export, her promotional billboard. It is the wealth of her 700 pubs in town (a world record).

Here also Arthur is king. Another Arthur of course, another kingdom than that of the round Table. When in December 1759, Arthur Guinness planted his tent, he met a landlord, of pure Irish turf, who was poet and optimist enough to lease him all of Saint James' district in exchange for an annual sum of 45 pounds, and almost indefinitely nine thousand years!

Today, as one faces the port that leads to the gigantic gardens of Phoenix Park, the Guinness warehouses block out the horizon from the port side of the Liffey, the Guinness-colored River!

The Liffey bisects Dublin. On the starboard, the right bank, lies the old historical part of town. Here is found the famous post office, scene of the national uprising, during Easter of 1916. Before landing, *Pêcheur d'Images* must first clear Customs House, a building more than one hundred meters (328 feet) long with Ionic columns, a Georgian façade and stucco ornamentation. A statue of the sea god Neptune

close to the Georgian Parks. From Merrion Square at one end to Fitzwilliam Square at the other, Dublin is a great town to walk through and is easily visited on foot.

Walking up the riverbank brings one to Temple Bar. It is impossible not to linger here awhile. Temple Bar is a very well known area, an Irish Saint-Germain-des-Prés in Paris or the Village in New York, where legendary artists such as Dublin figures Sean O'Casey or Brendan Behan have gone.

From Wellington Bank drift phantoms of Waterloo, but Arthur Wellesley, the Duke of Wellington was truly from Dublin…Temple Bar forms a rectangle crisscrossed with pedestrian streets leading to the old Parliament, to the castle and to Christchurch Cathedral. Not, however, to Saint Patrick.

The façades of the buildings are painted in bright colors. The colors and signs, all arranged in a straight line, tell of pubs and shops. As night falls, they light up like a string of festival lights.

In the district which inspired its name, The Temple Bar, the façades are blood red, the carpets green and the walls covered with frescos.

This is the traditional starting point for pub crawling, that ritual round of "public bars" better known as pubs. This is where you warm up like champions, a pint of beer or dram (a measure of whiskey) in

The port of Dublin is the lifeblood of Ireland. Today, a barometer of the country's economic growth lives day and night in the rhythmic movement of super tankers and ferries.

rises up to the copper dome. The boat glides along under the benediction of his protective arms.

The left bank is greener and livelier. When you leave O'Connell Street behind (named after one of the liberators of the nineteenth century), it's not surprising that this street is called Champs-Elysées. You go up to Trinity College. The university was created during the sixteenth century by Elizabeth I to spread anti-papist propaganda. The Irish elite, the Protestants first, were students of its hallowed halls.

Not far away is Saint Stephen's Green Square. It is a leafy haven

Ireland, Scotland and Brittany all have a surprising luminosity in the rain.

It is not rare to see them fight on the night of a Hen Party. In a race to get to the bar before the men, the women jostle each other shoulder to shoulder, glass against glass. Some furiously audacious, leave their maidenhood behind in a wild intoxicated whirl of alcohol and music. Fiddle and uileann pipe (a bagpipe played while seated with the help of an air filled bag pressured with the arm), follow the beat of the glasses of white wine, preferred by the pretty lasses to the harsh whiskey of the men.

Not long ago, the pubs were forbidden to women. A century ago, they would have been thrown out and threatened with the flames of hell. A strange Capucin Friar was in charge during that time of public morality. He came from the deep south of Ireland, from a parish in Cork.

In 1838, Father Matthew led a massive crusade against alcohol. He ferreted out and viciously condemned 21,300 backyard taverns and bars. Ireland who, in spite of herself, was attached to England, tried to drown her bitter collective melancholy with poitin, a powerful clandestine alcohol distilled at home.

On Saint Patrick's Day in 1841, Father Matthew celebrated his victory. After some years of virulent preaching, he had succeeded in persuading the British authorities to close down some ten thousand bars across the country.

On that day, Father Matthew baptized the "movement for total abstinence" and twenty thousand partisans of the holy water partook of his holy words in Phoenix Park, a short way from Bow Street, not far from the docks of Aran Isles. Ironically, it was here on the right bank of the river that John Jameson, pioneer of the whiskeys of Ireland, had dug underground wells in a lovely oak forest. The pristine waters from these

hand. Connoisseurs fight their way in, as though they were competing in the Olympics. Well, whatever the style, the essential thing is to participate.

When it is crowded, as it is every day, those who aspire to get to the bar sit on the sidewalk of Crown Alley with infinite patience, even the girls join in!

The literary pub with the glorious aura of four Nobel Prize winners lends prestige to these tourist attractions. Not a pub in Dublin hasn't had a figure of Irish literature at its bar at some time. And because every Irishman is a poet, every pub is a literary salon. This is known as the pub culture.

wells imbued his particular eau de vie with an unparalleled purity.

To this day, Father Matthew's movement still has its partisans. You may come across them wearing the badge of the Sacred Heart in their buttonholes. They camp outside bars and recite mocking verses condemning the drunken devils who, for the most part, remain supremely indifferent.

Father Matthew would be mortified were he to visit Smithfield Village today and wander the streets where in the past employees of Jameson's distillery lived in miners' terraced houses…There is Pass for Ceol, the museum of Irish music, but also Chief O'Neil's, a trendy café bar where you drink your whiskey along with small sea food snacks similar to Spanish tapas. Or The Chimney, a bar in a 60 meter (197 feet) tower offering its patrons panoramic views over Wicklow County. One can almost hear Father Matthew fervently reciting rosaries of "Vade retro satanas."

"Men only…"

Within the pubs, the time of male dominance is past and signs barring women from the main salon have become quaint antique objects.

It's a far cry from the vision of Father Mathew and the incantations of his anti-alcohol movement.

On the contrary, these days the women of Dublin have become the muses of these pubs.

Two movements have helped shape this Cultural Revolution: The first one is literary, the second musical.

The icon of the Irish literary pub has the impressive reputation among tourists of having been the spawning ground for four Nobel Prizes. Not a single pub in Dublin has ever been without the patronage of a well-known literary figure at its bar. Every Irish citizen is born a poet and every pub therefore becomes a literary salon. Inseparable

The social and cultural life of Ireland- magnified by its great museums, the National Gallery, Dublin Writers, Trinity College- is deeply rooted in its pubs. Indeed, it truly is the pub culture.

from the pub culture is the culture within the pubs.

Of course, some have the prestige of being able to boast the undivided loyalty of the most famous literary heroes. To every Lord every honor: The Brazen Head for instance, still in the area of Temple Bar, has been registered as a historical monument.

Its fine old oak walls with its lopsided staircase and low ceiling have watched history go by. Its license was ratified in 1666 by Charles the 1st thus giving it its noble stamp. It celebrated its 800th birthday in 1998.

Generations of patriots and rebels have raised their glasses here in memory of the *Wild Geese*; officers who gave their lives in service to the King of France after the defeat at the Boyne, in 1690.

It was largely those of the second generation who contributed to the victory of Fontenoy in 1745. A year later, they fell to the Scottish clans in the peat bogs of Culloden near Inverness.

They say that Wolfe Tone, a hero who was sacrificed just after the anti-English landed in 1796, braved the austere discipline of Trinity College. Daniel O'Connell, who was a monument of a man in Kerry, was himself a brewer and indeed the son of a brewer. He was an emblematic pillar to the community and subsequently became the mayor and liberator of Dublin.

In this climate, it's not hard to imagine Patrick Pearse and James Connolly, heroes of the bloody Easter uprising in 1916, secretly conspiring together at the Brazen Head.

Today, it is mostly declarations of love that are exchanged here and true to tradition, poetry is still recited passionately.

In this place, the ghost of James Joyce continues to roam conspicuously. The author of *The Dubliners* is also well known for his other masterpiece, *Ulysses*, which caused such a scandal during his time and was regarded as pornography. Today Leopold Bloom, the hero of the

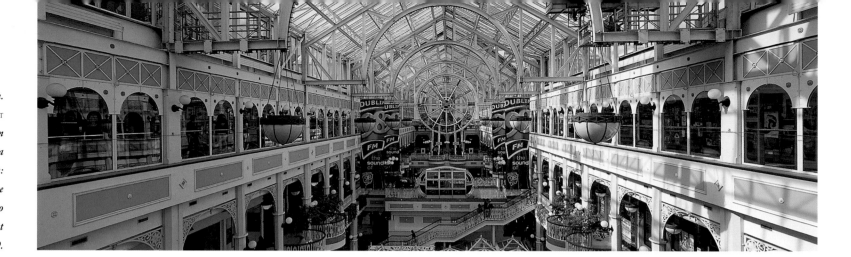

novel, lends his name today to an almost public holiday…The irony of morals in the shifting sands of time!

Along with Joyce, others like Sean O'Casey and especially Brendan Behan are members of Ireland's literary pub heritage. As for Yeats, he only made a brief appearance. Ah, but Brendan Behan! His statue thrones the entrance of that exclusive restaurant in Baggot Street, The Writer, with its chic and snobbish clientele. "I'm a Dubbalin man meself," he declares in a voluntarily contrived accent. It doesn't seem quite adequate in this sophisticated atmosphere.

There was once an Irish menhir: strong, warm, unruly and direct. He used crude language and had the reputation of being an eternal rebel. His commitment to the IRA (Irish Republican Army) and the years he spent in English prisons from the age of seventeen were the stock of his persona.

At the core of Brendan Behan's quick tempered and unyielding character, once the attraction of Parisian and New York cocktail parties, was a fountain of theater and literature. Poet, singer and heavy drinker, he let himself be buried by his drunkenness as did Jack Kerouac, his peer of the beat generation. The two most likely crossed paths in a wandering stupor in the Chelsea Hotel in New York. A plaque still commemorates Behan's last visit there in 1963.

He died a year later at age 40, still filled with dreams, passion and whiskey. The echoes of his laughter and raucous outbursts still resound though the pubs of Dublin. Even his fits of anger have become a part of the scenery. When Ireland awoke after his passing, hung over and with its heart at half-mast, The Clancy Brothers, the oldest of Irish

groups, composed their famous "Lament for Brendan Behan."

No stranger to life, he lived right enough
No stranger to the glass in his hand
No stranger to the cause he fought all his life
Yet they tell me bold Brendan is dead.

The only thing left to do now is to make your way through the rounds of singing pubs at night. O'Donoghue's, a few steps from Stephen's Green, is a lively address. This is Merrion Row, a chic example of the Dublin way of life, made trendy by its fashionable neighbor, the Shelbourne Hotel. Here tea is taken with people of good company and Guinness is drawn with the infinite patience of a Swiss watchmaker. No question of a pint being served without the symbolic emblem of the clover impressed on the head of froth. Irish folk music has made this pub a little musical Mecca. A guitar still hangs on the wall as a reminder of the day in 1962 when a redheaded elf, Luke Kelly, his hair burnt by the sun, snatched it up and played one of Ireland's best-known traditional airs: "The Rocky Road to Dublin," (since recorded by The Rolling Stones).

Everyone in the pub knew the words. In four verses, it took you from "Mullingar" to "The Boys of Galway" and the bad guys of Liverpool were chased out by music…

Ciaron Bourke, a 35-year-old bearded musician, passionate about playing guitar and harmonica, Barney Mckenna, mandolin and violin, and Ronnie Drew, guitar, violin and voice. All of them in their thirties,

they played with Luke Kelly till the early hours of the morning. Of course, they all made a toast to Brendan Behan and ended their session with a solemn IRA soldier's song. The historical hymn penned by Peadar Kearney, Brendan Behan's own uncle, which became the National Anthem. A band was born!

These four musicians first called themselves the Ronnie Drew Lads. Later, Duke Kelly who had read *The Dubliners* by James Joyce, decided on the simple but proud name, The Dubliners.

Three years later, the song "Seven Drunken Nights," one of a few they had written and dedicated to Brendan Behan, made it into the British Top Ten. They had recorded it in one take in three minutes. In the year 2000, youth is a state of mind…The Dubliners are still billed on posters for music festivals in Brittany but now without Luc, the fiery elf, who died in 1984.

All pubs in Dublin are venues for poets and musicians. Musical evenings are part of their traditional atmosphere and setting. Anyone can stage their own little verse or song here.

One of the most typical pubs is Mulligan's in the "holy" area not far from Trinity College and the Liffey River. This pub is not only a place of traditional shanties, its lounge is also the meeting place of the Organization for the Preservation of the Dublin Accent. Brendan Behan's colorful language surely rang out here on more than the odd occasion and the Dubliners have drunk here their fair share of "Whiskey in the Jar" – the title of one of the favorite drinking songs from their repertoire.

The Baggot Inn is a more varied venue. The tendency here is more towards rock and folk music. David Bowie, the Scotsman, and U2 have made their base here.

Another Irish rock figure is Sinead O'Connor. She has left her mark at the Bad Ass Café. This ex-model who charmed all of Dublin caused a scandal when she burned a photo of the Pope on American TV. Although it is difficult to consider her music typically Celtic, she recorded a moving version of "Foggy Dew." This song is a deep reminder

of the national Irish cause. One of the anthems of the uprising of 1916, it is a call to Irish soldiers drafted into the British army, risking their lives far from their country for the Union Jack and not for the tricolored – green, white, orange – flag of the rebels. "English difficulty is Irish opportunity." That was the slogan of the future Liberators. It surprised people to hear Sinead O'Connor speak of this.

A visit to Dublin will take you to many places by day, but more so by night. Sport is another main attraction within the city and shows you Dublin to be all at once young, tender and virile.

Croke Park is the temple of Gaelic Football, a sport played using both hands and feet. The two teams fight over a round ball but score goals kicking it between tall poles planted into the ground like rugby goalposts. Crowds of up to ten thousand fans come to see the game during the finals. These gatherings have sometimes produced such an

On the night of the Gaelic football finals in September, a second rush of crowds hit the pubs after the game. Whether they come from Cork, Limerick or Galway, the faithful drown their emotions in dark beer.

RIGHT

Statue of the novelist James Joyce on Earl Street.

atmosphere of national identity and conflict that in 1919, armed English troops fired on the crowd. The Croke Park field holds over twice as many fans as Landsdowne Road where football and rugby are played. The Cumann Luth Gaël, the Gaelic Sports Association, its emblem the harp and Celtic cross, generates a strong spirit of nationalism through the game and has played a large part in the wars for independence. Its anthem is still one of the old IRA marches: "A Nation Once Again."

On Finals night in September, a second rush of crowds hits the pubs after the game. Whether they come from Cork, Limerick or Galway, the faithful drown their emotions with black beer. Many meet at the Oval Bar half way along Abbey Street. The name of the bar refers to the shape of a rugby ball. On some days, supporters in kilts dance in front of the doors. They come to celebrate the victory of their heroes. But, don't be mistaken if you see red, yellow, navy blue and dark green tartans, united in a bouquet of flamboyant colors. These folk are not Irish, they are Scots of the MacKay, MacLean, MacDonald or MacLeod clans. With them, you would sing, "The Flowers of Scotland" rather than "The Soldier's Song." This is rugby day in Dublin.

It is understood, that the social and cultural life of Dublin, besides that of its big museums, National Gallery, Dublin Writers and Trinity College, is deeply rooted in its pubs. A whole world of literature, history, music and sport blossoms into a living fresco of memories and emotions that span a chain of generations.

It is time now for *Pêcheur d'Images* to weigh anchor. As Plisson heads south, a song is heard wafting over the water from one of the taverns. It is the plaintive song of "Molly Malone," the little fishmonger who died long ago from the fever. As always in Ireland, a pub's Bard – a Dubliner, a Chieftain, a Clancy Brother retraced the memory of a tender life long since gone.

"Molly Malone" sung every night, remains a symbol of the doomed times, like those of the Great Famine or emigration:

*She died of a fever
And no one could save her
And that was the end of sweet Molly Malone
But her ghost wheels her barrow
Through streets broad and marrow
Crying cockles and mussels alive, alive o!*

In 1988, a sculptor erected a bronze statue in her memory on Grafton Street.

In "Molly Malone" Dublin has found its muse.

Cape to the East

A STRAIGHT LINE, even by Irish standards, is the shortest route from one point to another. Both hikers and boatmen and women, love to travel west via the canals. The lock system spans a distance of 130 kilometers (80.78 miles) and is a perfect environment for Eco-tourism. After a few dozen locks, the Grand Canal flows into the River Shannon, the longest river of the islands across the channel.

Pêcheur d'Images is not a freshwater sailor and Phillip Plisson chooses to head out to sea. With the cape to the east, it's out onto the Irish Sea. The black waters of the Liffey soon turn to a dark blue.

But, somehow it's not so easy to leave behind the Dublin of James Joyce with the long narrow face, wearing spectacles and a tweed jacket and his ghost seems to follow in the wake.

The first lighthouse to starboard is a rather strange kind of beacon: The Martello Tower emerges above the coastal village of Sandy Cove. It was in this place, in the first pages of *Ulysses*, that Buck Mulligan camped at the summit of the rise and meditated over the ocean. Inspired by the fine mind if not the opulent body of Oliver St-John Gogerty, a Dublin surgeon and friend of Joyce's, the character recites knowledgeable thoughts whilst *overlooking the white bosom of the misty sea.*

Round and chubby, like the heroes in the novel, the Martello Tower is not attractive when seen from the coast. But to the curious visitor, it is a treasure trove with a thousand and one objects that belonged to the writer, even his guitar.

Standing at the gates of Dún Laoghaire (pronounced Leary, a fifth century king), the large ferry port shares its life with the hordes of tourists and the seaside weekenders from Dublin. They are drawn as though by a magnet to the charm of this mini Irish Riviera, adorned with azaleas and metallic hydrangeas.

Dún Laoghaire is an old fortified village on the east coast. With walls 12 meters (39.37 feet) high and 2.5 meters (8.2 feet) thick, the Martello Tower is part of a defense system built by the English in 1804.

They were worried, at the time, by one of the many threats of Napoleonic invasion. Of course, their angst raised a hope that spread amongst the dispersed rebels in different cultural Irish movements. A French boat exhibited in the Maritime Museum was brought back from Bantry – to the south of the island – after the failed landing of 15,000 troops in 1796. It remains a witness of the time when Ireland and France, like it was during the reigns of Louis XIV then of Louis XV, were allies against England.

But this is a technical stopover, a scenic detour. Dún Laoghaire was part of the ramparts of Dublin which became first a fishing port and then a port for pleasure boats. Here visitors dock their boat to taste the specialties of the aligned bistros facing the wharf: the Dublin Bay Prawn Cocktail and plates of bay scampi swimming in wine and whipped cream.

On the other side of the bay and nestled in the natural protection of its curve is the Baily Lighthouse. An attraction worth visiting, it blocks the horizon beyond Ireland's Eye, a rocky isle that seems to be taking off as hordes of silver seagulls protect their nests in the ferns.

A little farther to the north and already out of sight stands the Malahide Fortress. A visit to the fortress to salute its noble ancestry requires a trip along the Howth and Drogheda. Malahide was the estate of the Talbot family and was founded in the twelfth century. Loyal to James II, ally to Louis XIV, they fought together at the Boyne. Fourteen cousins would not come back. The ancestors of this line have been legendary heroes since 1690. The fortress remains open to visitors despite the death of the last Talbot in 1973.

Upstream, a few miles from here, the hooves of horses drum the sands of Laytown. It was here, less than a hundred years ago, that the Broach of Tara, which had been lost for centuries, was found. Perhaps thanks to the flick of a horseshoe. The broach is today one of the most beautiful of the golden jewels exhibited in Europe.

The beauty of Tara's broach arrests visitors in the National

FOR PAGES 28-31

The city of Dublin is indefinable. Many books could be written just about it. We have humbly chosen to portray its lights, colors and atmosphere, noted during our too short a stay.

The total of the grants attributed to navigation, with which 100 major lighthouses are managed, here, at the Irish Lights house headquarters.

RIGHT

Dún Laoghaire. A French boat is on display at the Maritime Museum. It was transported from Bantry after the failed landing of 15,000 marines, in 1796. It's a witness to the time when Ireland and France joined as allies against the English.

Museum in Dublin. Made of gold, silver, amber and enamel, it was once used to fasten the royal toga. The mythical site of Tara, capital of kings, where Laoghaire is buried standing in his armor, remains a place of spiritual and temporal worship. It was here that Daniel O'Connell, the mayor and "liberator of Dublin," in 1843, gathered a million people together to protest union with the English crown.

Every year when the big tides come between the end of July and the beginning of August, the beach at Laytown welcomes an unusual and noisy procession mounted on horseback in old-fashioned style.

One hundred riders compete over seven rounds in a 9 kilometers (5.59 miles) race on the golden and ash colored beach. When the tide ebbs far from the high water mark and the sand is left hard enough to gallop upon, a simple rope marks the racetrack with green and red pennants. The spectators laugh like children drunk with emotion and rush to share a free and intense moment of strong images.

The east coast of Ireland, unsheltered from buffeting winds, provides few strikingly serene images. Philip Plisson, at the helm of his trawler, fishes instead for other scenes, finding them on the Scottish coastline. Here, from Inverness to Peterhead and from Aberdeen to Dundee, abound a plethora of majestic and peaceful images.

Despite the apparent serenity, this is where Viking country begins. Of this history, Dublin has only preserved a picnic area in the shape of a drakkar and a bronze plaque under Ha Penny's bridge. But, by following this coast from Wicklow to Wexford, the smallish mountains in the background, one can easily imagine, as in a film, a great Nordic fleet spreading its square sails across the horizon. All through the ninth century, Vikings sailed this sea building trading posts and cities.

Today, its sweet climate attracts hordes of holidaymakers. At the foot of Glendalough's monastery and from the gardens of Powerscourt below Bray – the Irish Bournemouth – are a whole row of chic beach resorts animating this linear landscape.

After having studied the map, we search with our binoculars for the small town of Arklow, located halfway between Dublin and Rosslare. According to the holy legends of Ireland, this ferry port in

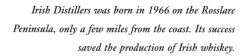

*Irish Distillers was born in 1966 on the Rosslare
Peninsula, only a few miles from the coast. Its success
saved the production of Irish whiskey.*

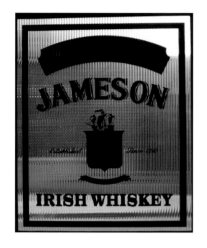

the southeast is where Saint Patrick first set foot when he came to convert the country in 432.

Those interested in magic (especially the magic of whiskey), will not miss the opportunity, if on the Rosslare Peninsula, to seek the foothills of the river that flows across Waterford County.

Somewhere in its valley, between Tourin and Cappoquin, stands Jameson's Manor. Kristin, the beautiful heiress, lives there with her hobbies: painting and breeding setters, majestic dogs in red Irish robes. It was her ancestors who created the first Irish whiskey. The motto on their crest is *sine metu* (without fear). They had won their noble title at the point of swords in naval battles.

Their coat-of-arms, a sailing ship, can be seen on the neck and the label of their whiskey bottles, which, in their turn, have sailed across the seas and conquered the world.

The sixties smiled, its music followed. England had The Rolling Stones and The Beatles; Ireland, the Clancy Brothers, the Chieftains and then the Dubliners and the Wolfe Tones, though rarely two at the same time…

With whiskey, there was Jameson and Powers, Paddy and Tullamore Dew. To each their own brand, all of them decorated with their own crest. Drinkers would be loyal to one and not the other… and one was recognized by one's colors. In Northern Ireland, it was even worse. Drinkers of Scotch whiskey and its local derivatives would block the way into pubs that served brandy from the south, regarded as Papist holy water by the penitents of the Holy Order of Orange.

Yes, the sixties sparkled with ambition and challenges and smiled on everyone. But not on to whiskey! Amber, black and golden beer had dethroned it.

So Sir Jameson, Kristen's father, convoked his peers. Their headquarters were founded in Dublin in 1780. Powers, in 1791, also in Dublin. Paddy, the pride of Cork distilleries, regrouped its five older southern brands, in existence since 1867. And finally Tullamore Dew, since 1829 the symbol of the two whiskeys of the land, couldn't just stand by.

People, therefore, found themselves in this manor, toasting a glass around a round table among commercial competitors, historical rivals and antagonistic families: *Slainté*…cheers…Some drams of rare, vintage reserved Jameson were produced and distributed in bottles decorated with rare Crested Ten or Redbreasts. A comeback slogan was found: Keep the Spirit Irish. This play-on-words around spirit and alcohol touched Irish hearts.

Irish Distillers were born in the shelter of the Rosslare Peninsula. 1966 marked, a few nautical miles away from the coastline where we crossed *Pêcheur d'Image*s, the rescue of Irish whiskey.

Southern Ireland opens like a page of sweetness with Kilkenny downstream, in this land that was once the ancient capital and cradle of the royal family. Yet even this place carries the stigma of English

Old Bushmill in Ulster is the oldest distillery in the world. Its license was granted in 1608. Today, Dave Quinn is living memory of the knowledge that mixes barley and water and perpetuates the originality of Irish whiskey.

It is here in Ireland that whiskey was born. The baptism of ancient Gaels with eau de vie comes from the monks returning from the Holy Land. Between prayers, they guarded their secrets of distilling. Barley and peat gave it a headier taste than the sweet fragrances of the Orient.

occupation. One district is still proud of having conserved the name Irish Town…Its population, pushed out of the heart of the capital, forged such a spirit of resistance that only Cromwell, with iron and fire, was able to reduce it, yet never completely snuff it out. By the very well known statues of Kilkenny, England had imposed the separation of the communities, effectively stopping Ireland from inheriting its cultural heritage. The Gaelic language was banned as a first measure…a medieval apartheid.

Kilkenny is surrounded by deep forests and rivers filled with pink salmon trout. A friend brought Phillip Plisson to Mount Juliet, a snug haven with its manor hotel and golf course designed by the champion, Jack Nicklaus.

It's fishing day. Better still, today there is a fishing competition. From amongst all of the Celtic peoples – 8 countries, one soul – the champions of fly fishing (an imitation insect camouflaged around a hook) will gather. Irish from Ulster or Connacht (Connemara, Mayo) and Munster (Cork, Kerry, Clare), Scots of the Spey or the Hebrides and even Welsh enthusiasts pull on their thick woolen sweaters and proudly display the badges of their club and symbols of their county.

Recognizable are the thistle of Scotland, the shamrock of Ireland. The red hand of the O'Neill clan has become Ulster's emblem and still present are the red lion of the past monarchs of Scotland and the Welsh dragon.

A three-legged figure embroidered on a red background could be confused with a Breton triskele, but this is the emblem of the Isle of Man, halfway between Scotland and Ireland, where the oldest Parliament of Europe has been sitting for the last thousand years. This figure utilizes the solar triskele which symbolizes the unity of the Trinity. Its motto declares: "Wherever it is thrown, it will stand straight." The emblem flies from the mast of the manor hotel between the Scottish saltire, Saint Andrew's cross and the Welsh dragon.

Beneath these fluttering banners, the champion of the day prepares to receive his prize for winning the competition.

No Breton ermine in the official scoreboard. But, by their presence, Philip Plisson and Christophe Le Potier, his second, bring an

Kilkenny is surrounded by deep forests and rivers filled with pink trout. Mount Juliet is a snug haven with its manor hotel and golf course designed by golfing champion, Jack Nicklaus.

Rosslare Peninsula is the crossroads
between the eastern and southern coasts.
The Saint-George Canal forms
a passage here between the South of the
Republic and Wales, joining the Irish Sea
and the Atlantic Ocean. This is the best
route to the North and is marked by
the lighthouse of Tuskar Rock, constructed
in 1815 after a ship foundered in these
treacherous seas.

The entrance to the Waterford River is
marked from one section to the next with
remarkable landmarks. On the starboard
side is the lighthouse of Hook Point, the
oldest in Ireland, constructed in 810 AD.
It was Irish monks in the sixth century
who lit and maintained the first fires here.
On the port side are three columns,
one of which is crowned with a metal
man, an original piece. This coastline,
like its estuaries, is rich in fish. Every
morning sees the ritual of the daily catch.

47

The port of Ballycotton looks like a movie set. It is protected by a little island crowned with a black lighthouse, one of the two black lighthouses in the Republic of Ireland.

SOUThERN CAPE

Cobh is a historical port town. A memorial to the sea and its sailors, it is the last harbor before America. 3.5 million Irish, fleeing war and famine, waited miserably on the docks here waiting for the maritime agent to call their name. The Cobh Heritage Center recounts through its collection of images, drawings and goodbye letters, the dark saga of families condemned to separation.

WE NOW FIND OURSELVES far from the crashing sounds of the seas that constantly lash at the Rosslare Peninsula. This crossroad between the eastern and southern coasts is named St. George's Canal. It forms a strait between the south of the Republic and Wales and unites the Irish Sea with the Atlantic Ocean.

This passage to the north forms the main maritime route to Scotland. This arm of the sea should have united Eric Tabarly and Philip Plisson, *Pen Duick* and *Pecheur d'Images*, Philip's trawler. They had made a rendezvous on the road to Fairlie, where the naval dynasty of architects – the Fife – had designed all those swan-like racing yachts.

Tabarly had committed himself to travel upwards to Fairlie, a prestigious place of yachting, nestled on the bank of the Clyde River as it flows harmoniously down to Glasgow.

While Eric Tabarly, with white sail and black hull, floats with the grace of his legendary namesake around Ouessant, the sentinel island of Brittany, Philip Plisson engages his *Pêcheur d'Images* around the reefs surrounding the entrance to Cobh (pronounced cove and meaning circus). His back is turned to the crescent shaped sandy beaches around Rosslare, its cliffs decorated with birds of the Saltee Isles, and faces the open skies.

Cobh is a museum port, a memorial to the sea and to sailors and is the last harbor before America. In 1897, before she added Oban, the pearl of the Scottish Highlands to the crown of her jubilee, Queen Victoria had taken over Cobh, with its soft and temperate climate, to the point of even dispossessing it of its Gaelic name. Up until 1920, Cobh was known as Queenstown, the town of the Queen.

It was during this period that 3.5 million Irish fleeing from guerrillas and famine, waited around its dock area in abject poverty, waiting for the agent to call out their name. Cobh Heritage Center relates the story in images and drawings, in goodbye letters and tabloid articles, a dark saga of families condemned to separation.

They put them aboard rowboats that took them to the coffin ships anchored out at sea. The shuttling of this Exodus began in 1838 when the *Sirius* first loaded up and bound for New York, made the crossing in eighteen days.

60 million Americans are of Irish descent. They call themselves Irish-Americans and their heritage stems from the emigrants of Derry, Belfast and Dublin. They were brought up singing Molly Malone's song from across the Atlantic, "Cockles and Mussels." The names of their families are exhibited at the Cork Museum like the credits from a *film noir*.

James Cagney, the young fighter of the screen and John Wayne, maverick hero of Wild West mythology. Maureen O'Hara, red-haired flame of Hollywood and Grace Kelly, Princess of Monaco and of the Oscars, are the children of the generations that made their escape in those coffin ships. Jimmy Connors and MacEnroe, the tennis players, Larry Bird, the basketball player of the Boston Celtics but also film maker John Ford and automobile inventor, Henry Ford and let's not forget the Kennedys. All of them belong in the pantheon of those who suffered a wretched exodus which metamorphosed into the springboard for a destiny of grace and glory.

Mel Gibson could also be one. The William Wallace of *Braveheart* encapsulates the role of rebels against the English Redcoats. There is a strong affiliation between the Irish and Scottish deported to Australia. Many were intransient adversaries of the Act of Union to The United Kingdom.

Coffin ships to America and Canada, prison ships towards

Australia, Queensland, Tasmania, New Zealand. The whole of an Irish population sailed aboard those ships, at the mercy of storms, looking for a friendly land that would welcome them.

And Cobh is also entwined with the story of *Titanic*. The history of Ireland is part of the disastrous destiny of that ship broken in two on an iceberg. It was built in Belfast in the naval yard of Howland and Wolf, and christened with demonstrative pride. It had the reputation of being unsinkable and Cobh was its last stop. Emigrants who embarked at the last minute here didn't know that the bell of their last hour had rung. They were amongst the third class passengers who were forbidden all access to the lifeboats.

Forty of the passengers who embarked at Cobh, were among the 675 survivors of *Titanic* (1,487 passengers died).

Cobh marine cemetery also remembers the ship *Lusitania*. She sailed between Liverpool, Cork and New York and was torpedoed by the Germans in 1915. When she sank, 1198 civilians died and 761 survived…Cobh has not forgotten any of its ghosts.

Neither has Cork for that matter. But here these dark ruminations evaporate in a visit to the pubs in Barrack Street. Pub crawling around Temple Bar in Dublin is nothing compared with the experience of the beer pubs here where the local black brew Murphy by far outsells the Guinness of Liffey and the whiskeys Paddy, Jameson or Powers from the capital.

Of all the rebellious cities, Cork (Corkain) even more so than Kilkenny and Dublin, was the heart of unstoppable rebellion. Its young mayor, Terence MacSwiney, an emblematic figure of the IRA, was arrested on August 12, 1920. He died on the 25th of October after 74 days of a hunger strike, shaming England from the stage of world opinion.

In reprisal, Cork was put to fire by the "Black and tans," a police force whose recruits consisted exclusively of orange patriots.

Cork remained the heartland and champion of all revolts and uprisings. It was the embarkation port of the Wild Geese, officers of James II who left after the defeat of Boyne and entered the service of the King of France.

Today, it is in Cork that ferries from Brittany set down their passengers. The most well known is *The Bretagne*. She is the pride of the ferries constructed in the Atlantic shipyards at Saint-Nazaire and now provides this privileged link.

But to the boat *Pêcheur d'Images*, Cork is also, and naturally so, the Royal Cork Yacht Club, the oldest yacht club in the world. Its inception dates back to the beginning of the eighteenth century. It was known then as The Cork Harbor Water Club but it no longer exists in Cork. Nor does the statue of Queen Victoria. They both lie buried under the ruins of history…

Cork is the Venice of Ireland and doesn't care about the destiny of the Royal Yacht Club. It was, in fact, transferred to Crosshaven a long time ago.

And even if the old building with its Italian architectural influence is no longer in vogue, the renovated Yacht Club organizes every two years a regatta keenly attended by holidaymakers: Cork Week.

From here Philip Plisson takes to the road in an 8 meter (26 feet)

Cobh is also the Titanic. The story of Ireland is tied to its funereal destiny that left her broken in two on an iceberg. Emigrants embarked at the last minute at Cobh not knowing that the bell for their last hour had rung. They were amongst the third class passengers and forbidden all access to the lifeboats. Forty of the passengers who embarked at Cobh, were among the 675 survivors of Titanic (1,487 dead).

Before Queen Victoria added Oban,
pearl of the Scottish Highlands,
to her crown in 1897,
she took possession of Cobh,
with its soft and temperate climate,
and even dispossessed it of
its Gaelic name. Up until 1920,
Cobh was known as Queenstown,
the town of the Queen.

Brow Head dominates Crookhaven. This is the last shelter
before Mizen Head, the most southwest point of County Cork.
You can see the tide ball flooding the Fastnet Rock.

Quiberon a year before, spontaneously joined the Irish *chouans*, their Celtic cousins. But, it is true that at this time England was their common enemy.

So 15,000 men joined the squadron to form a troop of audacious volunteers. Spread out over the fleet were one warship, 13 frigates, 7 battleships and a couple of corsairs experienced in battling the English.

Wolfe Tone was there in person on the *Indomptable*, a ship armed with 80 cannons. He bore the rank of executive officer.

"The Frenchmen in the bay!" is the chorus of an old song that schoolchildren still sing in memory of the event...

But a storm dispersed the fleet. Ten ships were sunk at the start of the engagement. It was a dramatic failure. Only ashes and tears remained. The *Surveillante* sank near the Island of Whiddy. It was scuttled. Red coats were everywhere. The surviving French were taken prisoner.

Only in 1980 was the wreck of the *Surveillante* brought up. Bantry has religiously kept the memory of Wolfe Tone and the love of the French alive. Side by side, the three-colored flags of Ireland and France fly above the façade of the French Armada Exhibition Center in Bantry House. The Castle of the Count of Bantry, especially the gardens of the south and "the staircase leading to Heaven" face the Bay opposite Whiddy Island where the *Surveillante* sank.

A pub in the old port bears the name of the ship, another the name of Wolfe Tone. A third posts a sign, "1796" like a crest. On the 14th of July, whiskey and Guinness flow continuously without French visitors having to pay a single Irish penny for it. With the ring of an eternally undaunted challenge, especially if there's an English ear around, people sing in chorus: "The French are in the Bay!"

Bantry piously keeps alive the faith of Wolfe Tone and its love of the French. The tri-color flags of Ireland and France fly side by side, fluttering in the breeze against the façade.

Bull Rock and Mizen Head mark the entrance to Bantry Bay.
In days gone by, families lived here to keep the coastal fires burning.
Ewes from the mainland were brought in to provide milk
for the children that were born to them.

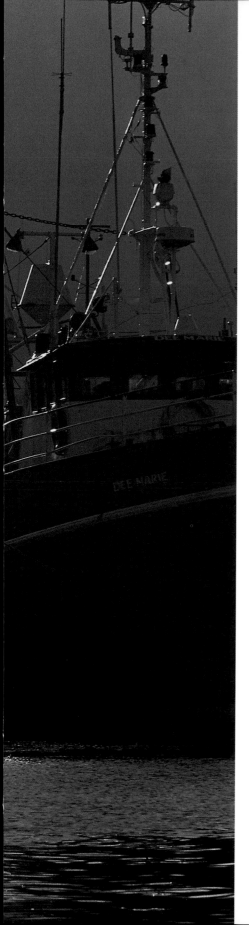

The castle of Dúnboy was formerly a manor. Today it is overrun with rhododendrons.

LEFT

Castletown Bere is a large, well-sheltered fishing port behind Bear Island
in Bantry Bay. It is the sister town of the Breton port of Locmiquélic in Lorient.
This is where the six lighthouses of southwest Ireland are found.
The pub/grocery store was where the keepers hung out.

The great western tide ball pounds its fist on the beaches of Bear Island.

FOR PAGE 82

The perfectly protected anchorage of Bear Island is a maritime heritage.

FOR PAGE 83

*As with many of the small villages here, the buildings and facades of Eyeries,
on the southern coast of the Kenmare River, are brightly colored.
Even when the weather is gray the streets keep a cheerful luminosity.*

Skellig, built on the flank of an invincible monastery, has been called "the most occidental fortress of Christ in the Ancient World." Perched above the waves like a rocky pyramid, the great Skellig rises 215 meters (705 feet) above the ocean, just a short distance from the aptly named Waterville.

FÓGRA

Tá an Séadċomarċa Náiṡiúnta ṡo
ṡé ċúram
Ċoimiṡinéiṗi na nOiḃṗeaċa Puiḃli
ċaṗ ceann an Stáiṫ do ṗéiṗ Aċṫ
na Séadċomarċaí Náiṡiúnta, 1930.
Iaṗṗṫaṗ aṗ an ḃpoḃal caḃṗú
leiṗ na Coimiṗinéiṗi ċun é ċoṗnaṁ.
Ẓaḃann pionós dian le doċaṗ nó
dioḃáil aṗ ḃiṫ do ḋéanaṁ do.

This National Monument
is in the care of
the Commissioners of Public Works
for the State under the provisions of
the National Monuments Act, 1930.
The Public are requested to aid
the Commissioners in preserving it.
Injury or defacement is severely
punishable by law.

OIFIG OIBREACH PUIBLI.
BAILE ÁTHA CLIATH.

The lighthouse of Valencia marks the narrow entrance of the river that flows to Cabersiveen.

LEFT

Portmagee, facing Valencia Island, is a small fishing port where tourists can take boat tours to Skelligs.

FOR PAGES 86-87

The lighthouse at Skellig Rock is automated today. Every month it receives its regular maintenance inspection. This is an opportunity for guests from The Irish Light to come and pay a moving visit to the only Irish monastery that has remained intact for a thousand years.

Sean is in charge of the life-boat on Valencia Island. As with all the Anglo-Saxon stations,
the budget (thanks to donations) permits these men to be full-time salaried employees.

RIGHT
Here, as is often the case, the sea is unforgiving. Their extensive organization is worthy of the elements.

Knight's Town is the main village of Valencia.

The pubs here are as lively as the colors of the buildings. This is an example

of its municipal fishing weigh station (topped off with a clock).

FOR PAGES 96-97

At low tide, Dingle Bay resembles the Bay of Mont-Saint-Michel in France.

Both places are known for the same specialty, salted mutton.

"**W**elcome to West Ireland. Kerry. Mayo. Galway. Sligo. These counties are filled with enchantment. Magic is in the air. Their common motto is "Lig duinn draiocht a chur ort." Let Us Put a Spell on You…

Beyond lies America.

Gallarus' oratory, a *clocháin*, a rectangular stone hut, has today become a spiritual retreat overlooking An Daingean, the Dingle Peninsula. It is the last promontory of the Irish coast and seems to barely resist the beckoning fingers of the ocean.

At its foot lie the Blasket Isles, the small country of Tomas O'Crohan whose name in Gaelic, O'Criomhtain, means the writer with calloused hands. A fisherman and farmer, he has given us *an t'oiléánach*, a masterpiece of simplicity and a transcription of life between oral tradition and the written legacy.

This work, first published in English in 1937, has since been published several times in different languages. *The Islandman* is to Ireland what the *Cheval d'orgueil* of Per-Jakez Hélias is to Brittany.

"O'Crohan," stresses his publisher, "is the spokesman for a culture that the English and all the drama of history have vainly tried to erase (…) With him, we sing, we drink, we row, we fight, we suffer, we forgive, we have miraculous fishing catches, we hunt the seal, the whales and the sharks, we discover the magic of the islands, the witchcraft of a civilization bathed in ocean mist, of poetry, of whiskey, of black beer, of music. And of humor."

The Islandman sings of liberty and the value of knowledge drawn from nature, humility and the grandeur of the human condition.

Flying in by helicopter and overlooking the waves crowning the six isles of the archipelago, setting foot on the first one of these, Philip Plisson could not overcome the malaise of a certain sense of déjà-vu…

In 1953, the last 22 inhabitants of Grand Blasket were "repatriated" by the government to the neighboring continent. For Plisson, this unfortunate scenario is a sad remake.

He reminds us, scene by scene, image by image and word for word of the forced evacuation of the inhabitants of Saint-Kilda in 1930. There were 37 people, 4 calves, 10 cows and the rest of a herd of unruly sheep difficult for the authorities to round up. Refusing to be uprooted from their wild prairies, some of the sheep threw themselves from the top of the rocks.

The Irish Blasket.

The Scottish Saint-Kilda.

Because of their difference in size, some sister islands can't be twins. Hirta, Stác, An Armin, Stác Lee – Islands lost in the Scottish seas with vertical cliffs rising 400 meters (1312 feet) and falling straight back down into the Atlantic. Stác Lee is a tooth of volcanic rock. They lie on the horizon, 100 kilometers (62.14 miles) from the furthest Hebrides. Hirta looks like a pyramid of rock like the Skelligs.

For 1000 years – one thousand! – A micro society, ruled by an autarkic community escaping British administration…the inhabitants shared essential crafts, fishing and hunting sea birds.

But the British administration didn't like these "celestial tramps" and one day the old ship, *Dunara Castle*, came cutting through the mist and took away the last MacDonald and MacKinnon of Saint-Kilda.

Their coup de grace was to spread this handful of inhabitants throughout the land of the Duke of Argylle, thus achieving "innocently" the demise of the memory of this clan.

The entrance to Dingle Harbor.

FOR PAGES 98-99

For a thousand years, a micro society controlled by an autarkic community, shared necessities, traded crafts and hunted Bassan sea lions. This was all done without resorting to any aid from the British administration. Inishteareght, the most remote isle of the Blasket archipelago, is home to the most remote lighthouse in all of Ireland.

The port of Dingle, in Dingle Bay, is the most naturally sheltered on the west coast. A very active fishing fleet operates from here.

When he landed by helicopter in 1998 to research his travel book, *Pêcheur d'Images in Scotland*, Philip Plisson found only the remains of thatched roof houses made from big dry stones. It reminded him of the clochain (small hut) of Dingle.

He photographed the plaque that UNESCO had erected there in 1987 – proclaiming this island as the heritage of humanity.

Saint-Kilda in 1930, Blasket in 1953, same destiny, same tragedy, the same harshness and tenderness shared in the holds of history.

Writers of these islands who bequeathed to us the memoirs of the Blasket Isles in an old Gaelic tongue are a joy to researchers: Mike O'Gaoithin, Peig Sayers, his mother and Maurice O'Súilleasháin (O'Sullivan in the Anglo-Irish way). All belong to the first half of the twentieth century. As Jean Bühler, one of the translators of Tomas O'Crohan O'Criomhtáin emphasizes: It wouldn't have ended with

Blasket if we weren't forced to fight to conserve their original purity.

As a matter of fact, a real estate investor, an American from California came looking around in 1986 and immediately set about establishing a foundation to protect the area. Unlike UNESCO at Saint-Kilda, it was not satisfied with putting up a plaque.

It created a national park on Great Blasket brushed by the winds and perfumed by the salty sea spray and you can hear the laugh of Tomas O'Crohan – *the Islandman* – ringing out under the stars.

How can one turn away from Dingle, its point and its isles, without saluting Ryan's Daughter? Robert Mitchum loved her in 1970 on the golden sands of Inch Beach, at the point of Slea Head. The entire village had been reconstructed for David Lean's cameras, on the coast where in 1916 the IRA used to come to pick up cases of arms.

The girls of Ireland, blondes, brunettes and redheads, all deserve to be appreciated like Mitchum did in the film. The obligatory passage at Tralee, the crossroads leading to the Shannon River, is like a Druid ritual at the end of August.

Tralee is nestled in the Bay. It is here that Saint Brendan, searching for the Promised Land, is meant to have set off in his curragh in the fifth century.

This monk was a great traveler. He visited Wales, Scotland and Brittany. He disappeared for seven years, a magical cycle. His disciples swear that he used this time to cross the Atlantic and discover the New World 800 years before Christopher Columbus. Philip Plisson also believes this. When he dedicated *Scotland* to Malo, his grandson, he wrote a "companion for Brendan the Navigator Saint, whose reports of the sea encouraged me to go further than my Breton horizons."

In 1976, another believer had the courage to construct, in the fashion of the first millennium, a curragh made of animal skin with a square sail, similar to those that still exist on the western islands. He followed the current that carried Brendan toward America…

At Tralee, romantic fiction is very close to reality, as it is everywhere in Ireland. They render homage to their patron saint in mid-May. At this time families come together and climb Mount Brandan, which dominates the Bay. The pilgrimage ends with singing in the pubs where storytellers and believers of the faith have heated discussions about religious doctrine and the visions of Saints.

Three months later, at the end of August, Tralee is filled with profane visions. With enthusiastic joy, they vote for the most beautiful woman in Ireland…in the world. From Savannah, in Georgia, America, to the villages of Queensland in Australia, the tough rounds of elimination trials lead to the final vote for that coveted title, "The Rose of Tralee." Here, Miss World is always Irish.

August is, by Celtic tradition, the month of the blessing of the sea. As in Paimpol in Brittany and Concarneau in the Bay of Cardigan in Wales, and along the banks of Scotland, a crowd uplifted by religious chants, surrounds the priests who resemble Druids with their hair flowing in the wind.

All along the coastal roads, from the round tower of Ardmore to forts dating back to the Stone Age…From Staigue, the proud southerner, to Dún Duchatair built on a promontory on the Aran Isles and up to the fields dotted with Celtic crosses showing the faith of the dearly departed, extraordinary treasures are found when "fishing for images."

The most colorful, the most rustic are found in the confines of Galway and Clare Counties. This is the home ground of the poet Yeats

from Sligo and the American filmmaker, John Huston.

We are at Kinvarra. The pier here is lined with fishermen's houses and the Cruinnu Na mBad are on display. This is an impressively large assembly of traditional boats, an entire armada of rustic boats and sailboats similar to the Breton coastal luggers, skiffs and the sinagots from Vannetais.

"Armada" is a loaded word here. The locals cross themselves when it is uttered. It is a reminder of the doomed fate of the fleet of Philip II of Spain, smashed against the cliffs of Moher during the terrible storm of 1588. Spain lost a lot in that debacle…Ireland, too.

Pressured by the English diplomats, the clan chiefs couldn't tell friend from foe.

The Invincible Armada was at the cross, as they used to say, and was the ally of Ireland. Their enemy was England.

When it set to sea, the objective of this proud and confident fleet of 130 vessels was to invade England from the south coast and bring down Elizabeth I.

There was more than religion at stake in this challenge by the Catholic King of Spain to Protestant Queen Elizabeth. Strategically, it would decide who ruled the Atlantic. The prize was the monopoly of the route to the colonies of the New World.

With their seafaring skill and aided by the winds, the sailors of Elizabeth I forced the Armada to head for Scotland. They would soon sail around Ireland. It was while coming down the west coast that they were beset by the storm. Wreckage. Debacle. Pillage. The survivors were massacred all the way into the hearts of the caves of Doolin.

God Save the Queen!

God had saved the Queen. All that was left now was to conquer

Loop Head marks the northern entrance to the Shannon River.
Here, the coast looks as though it has been cut with a knife.

These figures perched on the summit of the Cliffs of Moher, put the grandeur of this natural phenomena into perspective. It stands 216 meters (708 feet) high and stretching out over 8 kilometers (5 miles).

Ireland forever.

The ocean routes started in London. Rule Britannia: British Rule prevailed and almost without sharing the sea.

Of these tragedies, Ireland has kept a disheartened memory. The cliffs of Moher, spreading their abrupt majesty along several kilometers of coastline, still keep the stigma of the Invincible Armada.

Spanish Point is a few leagues away from these impressive façades of sandstone and black schist. But the children who sing their rhymes on the crest of the 216 meters (708.6 feet) high rocks, for a handful of Irish pence, never fail to add a sad couplet about the sailors who made the supreme sacrifice for Phillip II. We chase them away, like the

elves of *Riverdance*, down the paths covered in heath, around the majestic points at Hag's Head and Doolin where the greater part of the fleet sank.

The area surrounding Galway opens onto the great Gaeltacht, the largest region of Ireland where Gaelic is still spoken. It is sometimes the only language used on the road signs. Christophe Le Potier who is driving the motor home can't decipher them, even with his vague notion of the Breton language of his native

Morbihan. He needs a map. The Britonnic language, like Welsh, is a cousin of the Gaelic dialects of Ireland and Scotland.

Galway is the gateway to this. The last vestige of the wall that once surrounded the entrance to the medieval port calls out to you like a

Doolin, at the foot of Burren, is one of the small ports for the boats of the Aran Isles. The sea doesn't permit this trip every day.

distant reminder of the Invincible Armada.

The weather always plays tricks on Plisson. Rain and mist. Mist and rain. For four dark days, a storm in the city cuts like a claymore, the sword of the clan chiefs.

But a good *Pêcheur d'Images* never comes back empty-handed.

Life in the port becomes his new hunting ground. Its alleys are reminiscent of the disconnected cobblestones of Saint-Goustan, behind La Trinité-sur-Mer, at the end of the Auray River.

A place not to be missed is Kenny's Bookstore, a bookshop gallery with an Irish green façade where Kenny's family deals in treasures from the past.

One day Philip found a note stuck to his mobile home. Like a euphoric message in a bottle, it read: "I am Breton. I live here (the address followed). Long live the *Pecheur d'Images*. Come over. Ring the bell. And *degemer mat*…welcome."

Naturally, the evening ended at the pub. Galway, a crossing of rias and canals, the Venice of the West, city of all types of festivals, literature, art, film, and horse riding, the oyster festival…A city that's never dry.

Tigh Neachtain, near the quay, is a good place to go for the first round. The piano has seen better days but tonight there's a live band. Tin whistle (a small enchanting flute), a bodhran, a tambourine and uileann pipe (a bag pipe played sitting down) set the mood for the evening, which turns quickly into an Irish *ceili* (pronounced kaylee), an informal and graceful popular ball.

The second round is on the other bank, behind the Wolfe Tone Bridge. Monroe's Tavern is packed, as usual. We end up next door for the third Round at Roisin Dubb, where the music flows like beer.

It's now, round after round, that you keep up the atmosphere as if in a contest of brilliant word and wit. Ireland is famous for playing with words – like the "true" legend of the Dog of Galway.

Everyone here knows that Christopher Columbus made a stopover in Galway before heading off to the Indies, which were in fact, America. On his way, he picked up a dog that was hanging around

Galway is worthy of a long stopover. It's the starting point for visiting Connemara. Life here is centered on the port and the university.

the port. When they finally approached land, the setter literally jumped across the last stretch of water and reached the New World before Columbus…

Come on, one last round. *Slainté*, cheers to Columbus. After more rounds, the beautiful Bretonne stranger and her young Irish husband, fans of *Pechêur d'Images'* photos, make Plisson an Honorary Citizen of the Old Port. In this atmosphere, even Trinité-sur-Mer becomes Shamrock-sur-Mer… Philip swears that he will take back to

his son-in-law, an oyster farmer, the recipe for oysters à la Guinness, the specialty of the Spanish Arch.

Ireland is a country of storytellers. It loves to recount stories of sailors. The Galway Tourist Office has put the following into one of its brochures:

"Tired and hungry, a yachtsman headed for a small port in the west. When he arrived at the quay, a man approached him and said: "My wife and I saw how difficult it was for you to reach port. So, we prepared a hot bath and dinner…"

This anecdote underlines the quality of hospitality that is the pride of Ireland. Some people may think this to be a myth, like the stories of Epinal (traditional or historical anecdotes from eighteenth century France) or clichés that have since become banal.

Philip Plisson swears that it's true. Whilst he was heading out to the Aran Isles onboard a helicopter, another passionate photographer of the sea hailed him.

"Come on over and have dinner at my house tonight."

"Thanks, but we're leaving for the islands. Sorry…"

Two days later when they returned, Philip and Christophe found a basket full of lobster and scampi in front of their mobile home.

What their unknown host would have offered them at his home – he left for them at their place.

In Galway port, boats tie up and the crews head for Padracins, a pub unlike others; it's open 24 hours a day. The musicians here are like the boat crews. They move to the rhythm of the port.

LEFT

Comas O'Riada is a lively musical pub in Galway. Here musicians of all origins play together every night.

114

*By November, the days are already short but
nature here can still create a picture of rare beauty
such as this one of fishing boats returning
to the port of Rossaveel at the base of Aran's Island.*

Inis Mór, Inis Meáin, Inis Oírr: The Aran Isles.

Here you say, *Dia duit* for good morning, and *dia is muire duit* (pronounced: djay a maha ditch) for good morning in return.

A pint, please, is an important password. Those at the jetty say, *Pionta, le do thoil* (pronounced: pinne teuh lèdeu heulle)…

You will have noticed that the Aran Isles is a center for the preservation of the Gaelic language, as is the Isle of Skye in the Scottish Hebrides.

Inis Mór (Inishmor) is the largest of the Aran Isles. It is thirteen kilometers (8.08 miles) long and three kilometers (1.86 miles) wide. The other islands are smaller and rounder. They are located 45 kilometers (27.96 miles) from Galway and thirteen (8.08 miles) from the coast of Connemara. The plane ride from Galway to Inis Mór takes only six minutes. Even so, ferries still serve the three islands, from Galway and Doolin. They come and go under the cliffs of Moher.

To each his own, whether that be pier or aerodrome.

Seen from the sky, these islands are made up of low walls and pocket-sized fields and resemble a vast checkerboard of ash, green and sometimes blue, like stone lacework.

John Synge wrote *The Aran Island* at the beginning of the twentieth century. His book inspired the Irish-American filmmaker, Robert Flaherty. In 1934, *Man of Aran* brought to the screen the precarious, dignified, courageous and often risky life of these insular families jealously guarding their heroic isolation. Many visitors, attracted by the archaeology, the forts (dún) and the flora, are still moved by the strong and poignant images of the *Man of Aran*, in which all the characters are played by the inhabitants of the island, in real-life situations. Here, women still wear a red skirt with a single fold if they are single, two

*Vessels making for Galway from the south travel along
the starboard side of Inisheer, the smallest of the Aran Isles.
Its lighthouse marks the channel with the mainland.
More than one boat has run aground on the coast here.*

122

folds if they are married, and three if widowed.

In Kilronan, this film in black and white is shown for visitors three times a day, just two minutes away from the steps of the jetty, near the Heritage Center.

Philip Plisson's helicopter takes one last sweep around Dún Aonghasa, the fort of Inis Mór. Surrounded by the remains of walls in a half-circle, it crowns the cliff with its swarms of guillemots (black and white diving sea birds).

He now heads down to the lighthouse of Inís Meáin, the younger island, cradled between the two others. And finally we begin our approach to the temple at Inís Oírr – the roundest and smallest of the islands – dedicated to Saint Kevin, its ruins covered with sand in the dunes. After a few minutes, Philip Plisson was able to get a perfectly aligned shot of the sister islands.

On the water below, a line of ochre hooker sailboats and wooden curraghs with their tarred canvas, powered by a trio of rowers, passes by. It reminds one of the times when Saint Brendan walked on the water. They too glide over the waves instead of dividing them. A light-hearted fisherman perhaps heading back from the continent; from Claddagh, there where wedding rings are made of fine gold in the form of a crowned heart. The wedding ring of Claddagh is a token of love. To wear such a ring is the dream of girls from Clare, Connemara and Mayo. If it comes from Claddagh itself and not just any ordinary shop in Dublin, it is a symbol of faithfulness.

From wild ponies to mauve taxis, the bitter but enchanting country of Connemara is left behind, its gates leading to Clifden.

On the way they pass through Rossaveal, another fishing village and harbor for curraghs, propped up against the gulf.

This totally mineral world is seen when flying over Inishmore. The forts of Dún Eochla (opposite page in the center) and of Dún Aonghasa (opposite page on the right) are defenses that date back to the Bronze Age.

FOR PAGES 120-121

Seen from the sky, Inishmaan and Inisheer, with their network of low walls, resemble a vast checkerboard of ash and green with bluish threads running across it like stone lace. At their base: the Cliffs of Moher.

The season ends for the hookers.
In the small port of Gorunna Island,
the fleet waits to be laid up.

FOR PAGES 130-131

The Carna Peninsula:
A father and his son aboard their currragh.

Thatched roofs, hookers and curraghs,
such are the colors of Connemara.

FOR PAGES 132-133
For decades, the English Crown forbade
fishing along the Irish coast.
Today, the harvest of this artisan activity
is exported to France and Spain.

Green Kerry, green Clare and green Connemara…Slowly and little by little, the colors turn browner. The sky and the valleys become more austere. The road follows isolated coves all along this coastline, the most jagged of all Ireland. You can feel the eternal struggle of the "Finistere," (the end of the world) here land meets the pounding of ocean. Every harbor is carved with caves, like pockmarks in the skin of the cliffs. Every cave holds the memory of a hiding place for rebels and smugglers. The pirate queen, Grace O'Malley, once ruled this torn up territory.

Achill Island is the biggest island of the Irish Isles and also the most barren. As with the Burren area, a lifeless, lunar landscaped countryside between Clare and Connemara, the quote of one of Cromwell's officers is apt: "This is a region where there's never enough wood to hang a man and not enough earth to bury him."

At least, there's enough water (the sea) to drown him…

Here, the sky changes every day to the rhythm of accelerated seasons. Philip Plisson watches and waits for blue sky to emerge from under the cover of sudden black clouds, a clearing after the storm.

After a trial of wind, currents and counter-currents, Clare Island in Clew Bay appears and offers a welcome respite for the boat just as the storm lifts. The lighthouse here doesn't work anymore. It's been converted into a Bed and Breakfast. The owner comes down in his Land Rover. Welcome. There are still twenty minutes of rocky road to go. A couple of Americans are already there. "Hello, how do ya do?"

One after the other, we walk into the lighthouse that now has become a guesthouse. Introductions are made and we all have a drink.

The Americans – professors from Massachusetts – are on their honeymoon. They have Plisson's best-known photos at home. Promise.

Monica Timmermans' Bed and Breakfast is the former lighthouse of Clare Island. Its lights can be seen from Achill Island. (opposite)

In autumn, storm fronts come in from the Atlantic
as fast as the wind letting through rays of ephemeral light.

FOR PAGE 140-141

Achill Island is the largest island of the Irish Isles
and also the most barren. Referring to this lifeless, lunar landscape between
Clare and Connemara, the quote of one of Cromwell's officers is apt:
"This is a region where there's never enough wood to hang a man
and not enough earth to bury him."
At least, there's enough water (the sea) to drown him...

Westport, Newport, and Mulrany languish in front of the isles like a rosary surrounded by golden beaches, calm lakes, and somber mountains. Saint Patrick keeps watch over this coastline, rich in the nostalgia of its Anglo-Irish past.

The summit of Croagh Patrick, the highest peak in the country, reaches 765 meters (2509 feet) above Clew Bay. It's here that Saint Patrick, according to legend, destroyed the serpents of Ireland.

The mountains are blanketed with an abundance of heath and fuchsias in this protected microclimate. So, Saint Patrick is honored with flowers all year round.

Still, this doesn't stop the thousands of pilgrims who come at the end of July from covering his statue with floral ornaments.

Like King Arthur, armed with Excalibur the golden sword, watching over his Celtic Kingdom from the top of the Eildan Hills in Scotland, Patrick protects Ireland. Behind is the county of Mayo, where the French landed in vain two years after Bantry. Then Sligo, the Donegal – Dún Na nCall, the fort of the foreigners – and of course Ulster…another cross for Saint Patrick to bear.

When the wind whips in from the northwest and becomes a storm, nature puts on a spectacular show.

Unfortunately, because of the conditions, there's no one in the photo to give an idea of its full dimension.

Man and beast alike have learned how to protect themselves from the wind.

144

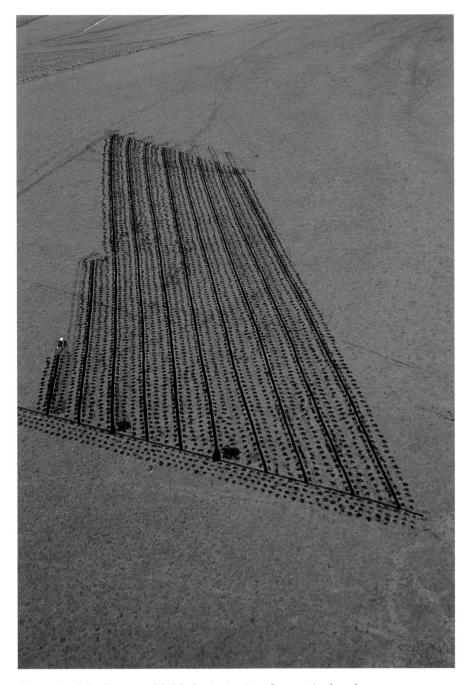

Peat remains Ireland's most used fuel for heating in winter. Its extraction has taken on an industrial character.

The coast is also a cemetery for boats.

The metal man points the way to the entrance of the port of Sligo.

This last big bay on the west coast between Sligo
in the north and Donegal in the south is
a marvel of clear water reminiscent of the Caribbean.

CAPE TO THE NORTH

1798 IT WAS YESTERYEAR, but in reality it's not so far away. France, lifeless, was coming out of the Terror. And in spite of everything, in the eyes of revolutionaries, she was like a beacon. The Irish believed in the strength and support of the French to drive out the English once and for all.

Like a gull in a storm, Wolfe Tone still dreamt of hovering over the masts of a vessel.

Slim and dashing in his uniform as head of the brigade, he was part of the *Directoire*. Two years after the debacle of the Bay of Bantry, he no longer had the ear of General Hoche or Humbert, whose hands were full with the wars of the Vendée, as were Lord Cornwallis' during the American War for Independence. Today, Cornwallis holds Ireland under the hoof of his horse.

Bantry…The peasants of Kerry lamented that it was the Protestant winds that threw the French into the sea.

Wolfe Tone insisted that the North coast, around Sligo, was the easiest way in. He swore that a united Irish people, the Fenians, his party, awaited only the appearance of one French sail to rise up… Catholics and Presbyterians would march in step together as one…He himself a Protestant was living proof of it…

The *Directoire* secretly dreamt of plucking the British crown with the point of the Irish clover.

"You are a brave man!" cried Hoche. Tone had won.

The French fleet had, tragically, drifted in the waters of the South and so they came up the west coast, bypassing Galway and heading for Sligo and the Cape to the North.

Humbert and Wolfe Tone were soon stranded in the harbor at Kilcummin.

They had already brought in the sails of three frigates. One thou-

sand men and the seventy officers who led them rushed to get their boats out to sea.

One thousand men! What devastation. It brings to mind the tragedy of the forces of Bonnie Prince Charlie, heir to the Stuarts, thrown into the Scottish seas with his followers fifty years earlier after the Culloden disaster.

It was the twenty-second of August and instead of a national uprising, it was "a band of peasants, lead by wrestling champions and some fox hunters," who rallied to the French. And although they were a heroic bunch, they were disorganized and untrained.

Killala borders one of the pristine beaches of Mayo. On the twenty-fifth, it was taken: Five thousand English foot soldiers and one thousand cavalry flee.

But Cornwallis rallied his men…

So began the "Year of the French." Its tragic memory still haunts all of Mayo and Sligo, all the way up to Donegal and still burns in the hearts and minds of the people here.

When, in his turn, Philip Plisson landed at the peat bogs of Killala and Ballimanuck, where the Irish green turns to a deep brown, he stirred up ghosts that have never really left these places.

Thomas Flanagan, an Irish-American university professor, spent ten years reconstructing their painful and romantic saga and he has recounted the historic events with Malcolm Elliott (attorney and member of the United Irish Society):

"Our lines stretched the length of a meadow. Bartholomew Teeling (member of the United Irish Society and an officer of the General Staff of Humbert) on his elegant bay mare, sabre in his fist, followed by a small group of French cavalry, assembled the Irish troops (…) The French beat their drums and cannons roared (…)"

"Okay, forward to the slaughter house," shouted MacDonnel, who was a horse breeder as well as an officer in the rebel army.

"After the victory of Collooney, they marched until nightfall leaving behind them the frightened, silent hamlets, hidden away at the crossroads, where the river bends (…) The drums of the French, like

At the extreme northwest of Ireland, in a labyrinth of islands, a little fishing port in the authentic village of Bunbeg is particularly well sheltered from the biting Atlantic.

cavernous heartbeats, counted out the cadence for the march. His throat dry, MacCarthy (poet and soldier) was thirsty for whiskey, milk and mint."

Finally, Elliott recounts, "the slow and inexorable destruction of the first "Republic" of Ireland in the sinister landscape of the peat bogs of Ballimanuck."

"(…) The trumpet of Crauford (commander of the English dragoons) sounded a fanfare indicating that all resistance had ceased on the hill (…) I looked at Humbert. He handed his sword to Crauford who raised his fingers to his hat before accepting it."

This tragic ending sent Humbert to prison and Wolfe Tone to his death, his throat slashed in prison. He is cited in the Irish Requiem. This has had a marked effect in the North – six out of nine counties in

The lighthouse of Tory Island is in the extreme northwest of Ireland. The wall around it is designed to protect the keepers from the roughest storms. John Joseph Doherty, who has kept the fire burning here for more than twenty years, visits monthly. The people here speak Gaelic and have their own hallmark.

155

The calm waters of Lough Swily, in the north of Donegal, are lit up on the left bank by Fanad Head Lighthouse. This lighthouse, constructed in 1817, is the training base for the personnel of The Irish Light for lighthouse maintenance in all of Northern Ireland.

Ulster (Fermanagh, Tyrone, Armagh, Down, Antrim and Derry) – remain under the law of the Protestant majority whose rival fundamentalist factions compete to see who can be the most loyal to London.

Objective: Errigal Mountain.

Situated a little lower than Croaigh Patrick, it's the highest point in Donegal. One can see as far as Scotland on the starboard side and over to the mountains of Connacht overlooking Sligo. This is Yeats' native land; he describes its landscapes in some of his poems. The view here spreads over Mayo, Roscommon and the foothills that protect Galway. It embraces the entire province of Connaught.

At the foot of the mountain is the Inishowen Peninsula and Tory

The lighthouse on the left bank of Lough Swily, in this mountainous region, the Dunree Lighthouse guides vessels entering and exiting the fishing port of Rathmelton which is particularly well sheltered.

Island. Swept by the winds and lined with ash, it is the poorest island in the world. The patron saint of this island is Saint Columban and its pagan saint, its bright red sunsets, a joy to the local painters.

It is winter.

Philip Plisson decides to brave the cold. It is minus fifteen degrees Celsius (5 degrees Fahrenheit). He points his mobile home toward the hills of Errigal in his eternal quest for the Holy Grail of photos.

Night falls quickly.

Not only is the sun, be it red or white, absent at this rendezvous but the mist hides the moon.

Suddenly, in front of a rest area which shelters a statue of the Virgin, the mobile home skids on some ice and ends up in a ditch… Christophe and Philip are in trouble. The cold cuts through their clothing. While they try to keep warm in their parkas, the ice starts to freeze the wheels of the mobile home.

It is already 11 PM. Night transforms this adventure into a snowy wasteland of anxiety. Using his mobile phone, Philip takes a wild guess and dials what he hopes are the emergency numbers: 111… 222… 333…And then, suddenly there is a voice. It's a miracle! The police from Gweedore, a village right next-door, answer.

At three o'clock in the morning, two farmers, like ghosts from Killala and Bullimanuck, appear out of nowhere. They are driving an imposing tractor and although relieved at the sight, Philip feels very embarrassed. The volunteer rescuers quickly sweep away his chagrin by bringing out their thermos bottle.

They get warm with a "hot Irish," the soothing hot whiskey drink. The farmers sing "Dongegal Danny" to ward off the cold. This classic of the Dubliners is a favorite in the County.

On the other side is Derry. The other Ireland, as they call it modestly, beats with a heavier heart.

Since the Treaty of London in 1921, all world maps represent the Free State of Ireland in green. Ulster (reduced now to six counties out

Malin Head is the northern most point of the mainland. Inistrabull is its extension. The new lighthouse, kept by Donal O'Sulivan, is constructed on the last inch of soil within the Irish Republic. From here you can see Islay Isle and the south of Scotland.

The lighthouse of Inishowen overlooks
the approach to Londonderry.
On the other side is Derry. This other Ireland,
as they modestly call it, beats with a heavy heart.
Since the Treaty of London in 1921,
maps all over the world represent the Free State
of Ireland in green and Ulster,
allied with Great Britain, in a uniform orange.

Redcastle is a seaside resort and active fishing port on the left bank of Derry.

of nine, the exceptions being Cavan, Monaghan and Donegal), allied with Great Britain, is represented in a uniform orange color.

The Orangemen have made the law for five centuries. Green was banned not long ago. Since 1968, Derry, coiled at the base of the Foyle River, has relit the flame of insurrection. Urban guerrillas have found their place once again in the pages of history.

William of Orange and Thomas Cromwell made Derry a stronghold and the plantation colonists, coming for the most part from London and the lowlands of Scotland, changed its name to Londonderry. After the victory of the Boyne near Drogheda in 1689, the siege of Derry signaled the death knell for James II and his followers, the Jacobites. Over the course of the last five centuries, the outcome from these two feats of arms have written painful pages in the book of a divided Ireland.

The 12th of July is a day of confrontation. To the sound of fifes and tambourines, marching Orangemen come looking for a fight at Bogside, where the Catholic community lives.

Modern history is just a succession of mourning. January 30th, 1972 (when 13 people died after being mown down by the British army) remains sadly embedded in the memory of the people as "Bloody Sunday." Paul McCartney, the Celtic Beatle, wrote a ballad with the message: "Give Ireland Back to the Irish." It was banned from BBC airwaves.

Strange and crazy Northern Ireland! The myth of Finn Mac Cool (its hero) is still trying in vain to bring together the two bigoted and antagonistic populations. Do they really believe in his legend? According to it, he was in love with a pretty Scottish giant who clung to the cliffs of Staffa, a neighboring island close to the peninsula of Mull of Kintyre. With bagpipes playing in the wind, McCartney put to music the spellbinding beauty of this peninsula.

To be reunited with his true love, Finn Mac Cool is said to have constructed a huge underwater road. Thus was created Aird Snout, the Giant's Causeway, or the Giant's Harp because of the way the waves smash against the rocks.

This geological coastal formation is classified as part of the Patrimony of Humanity. Flying over it in his helicopter, Philip Plisson thought it looked like a great geological opera of thirty seven thousand

FOR PAGES 166-167 AND LEFT

The Giant's Causeway is a marvel of nature.
37,000 columns of basalt sculpted
and eroded by the elements give the impression
of an immense bee's nest.

BELOW AND RIGHT

Torr Head is a natural frontier. It is the closest
point to Scotland, separated by North Canal.
Here is seen the Kintyre Peninsula,
one of the greenest grazing regions of Ireland.

columns of basalt that form cliffs and plateaus sliding beneath the sea.

Opposite is Staffa answering in a different symphony, more modest with volcanic organs sounding their legendary dimensions.

And then there's Belfast…The modern naval shipyards have replaced the old warehouses of Howland and Wolf, where *Titanic*, like Finn Mac Cool, was born of delusions of grandeur. Much work is being done to restore the rustic dockyards that flank the Lagan River as was done so well in Scotland with those in Glasgow on the Clyde River. There, every modern activity takes place around the old docks. Architects take on artistic challenges, the best lofts are fought over and the merchant's galleries are crowded with crowds happy to spend… such are the dreams of the promoters of a new Belfast.

Here too, as in Derry, the ultras of each community live sheltered in barricaded neighborhoods. Falls Road, a Catholic area is filled with murals painted all over their houses glorifying the IRA. On the other side, the loyalists of Shankill Road make their answer with desperate oaths of loyalty and submission to the Queen of England.

New dreams of peace awaken however, at Stormont, the austere and grandiose Parliament of Northern Ireland.

One day, perhaps in the dawn of the Third millennium and certainly not before we will see the lads of Falls and Shankill roads exchanging their Jameson's and their Powers, made in Dublin, for a Blackbush from Bushmills Distillery, oldest in the world (1608) installed at the Giant's Causeway.

At the Crown pub, the oldest in Belfast and in all of Ireland, we will raise our glasses to the health of Saint Patrick. On that day, 'tis sure, he will truly have performed a miracle.

WELCOME TO THE MOST TALKED ABOUT BAR IN THE WORLD WWW.BELFASTTELEGRAPH.CO.UK/CROWN

EST: 1849

The Crown Liquor Saloon: This luxurious Victorian bar first opened in 1880. Its décor is a mixture of stained glass, marble and mosaic. Here you can sample one of Ireland's specialties…oysters served with a pint of Guinness.

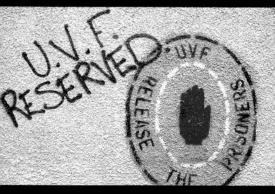

The east coast of Ireland is protected from prevailing winds
and is made up of many bays and natural ports.
Fishing and maritime transport are its principal economic activities.

FOR PAGES 174-175

Fanatics of each community live sheltered in barricaded neighborhoods.
Falls Road, a Catholic area to the west, is filled with
murals painted all over their houses glorifying the IRA. On the other side,
the loyalists of Shankill Road make their answer with
desperate oaths of loyalty and submission to the Queen of England.

We conclude our 3,000 kilometer (1,864 miles) journey around the large island with its four lighthouses on the way to Dublin. It was here in Ireland that the first lighthouses were lit and today they have punctuated our journey and are the symbol of a rediscovered unity. And it has been from Dublin that the commissioners of Irish Light have managed and administered all of the lighthouses of Ireland. Truly, a ray of hope.

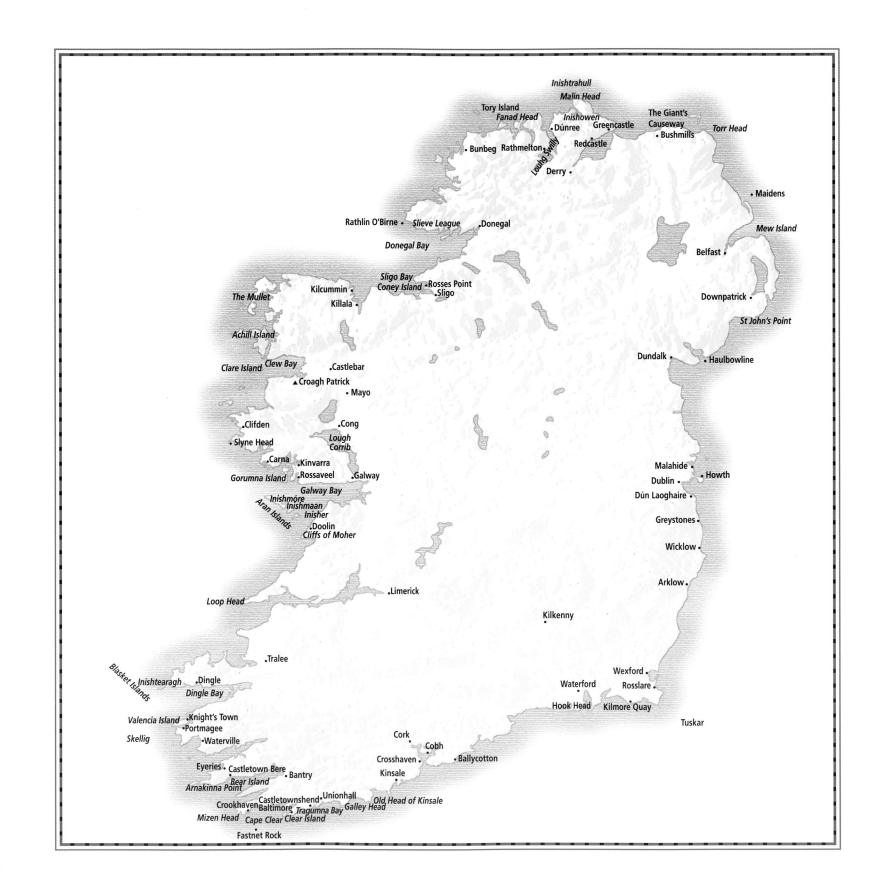

Inishtrahull

Malin Head

Tory Island
Fanad Head   The Giant's
                    Inishowen   Causeway
                    Dúnree   Greencastle   Torr Head
        Rathmelton   Redcastle   Bushmills
Bunbeg

                    Derry

                                                        Maidens

Rathlin O'Birne   Slieve League   Donegal   Mew Island

              Donegal Bay   Belfast

                    Sligo Bay
         Kilcummin   Coney Island   Rosses Point   Downpatrick
The Mullet   Killala   Sligo
                                                        St John's Point
Achill Island
                                                        Dundalk   Haulbowline
Clare Island   Clew Bay
                    Castlebar
        ▲ Croagh Patrick
                    Mayo

     Clifden   Cong
                                                        Malahide
Slyne Head   Lough   Dublin   Howth
                Corrib
        Carna   Dún Laoghaire
              Kinvarra
Gorumna Island Rossaveel   Galway   Greystones
              Galway Bay
              Inishmór   Wicklow
              Inishmaan
Aran Islands   Inisher
                Doolin   Arklow
              Cliffs of Moher

                                   Limerick

Loop Head
                                   Kilkenny

                    Tralee
                                                   Wexford
Blasket Islands   Rosslare
    Inishtearagh   Dingle   Waterford
        Dingle Bay   Hook Head   Kilmore Quay
Valencia Island Knight's Town   Tuskar
            Portmagee
Skellig   Waterville
                              Cork
                              Cobh
                    Crosshaven   Ballycotton
    Eyeries   Castletown Bere   Kinsale
        Bear Island   Bantry
Arnakinna Point   Unionhall
      Crookhaven Castletownshend Old Head of Kinsale
        Baltimore Tragumna Bay Galley Head
Mizen Head Cape Clear Clear Island
        Fastnet Rock

180

INDEX OF PLACE NAMES

A Thousand Leafed Clover

Even if the clover incarnates the Holy Trinity, it is, above all, a symbol of Ireland. A four-leaf clover is a symbol of luck. Irish literature and the literature dedicated to the Gaelic Isle hasn't stopped growing. Here's a harvest of interesting books. A thousand leafed clover...

NOVELS

The Year of the French, Tomas Flanagan, ed. Arrow Books

The Dubliners, James Joyce, éd. Bantam Classic and Loveswept, 1990

Ulysses, James Joyce, éd. Vintage Books, 1990

Les poneys sauvages, Michel Déon, éd. Gallimard

Le taxi mauve, Michel Déon, éd. Gallimard

The Islandman, Tomas O'Crohan, éd. Oxford University Press, 1978

Inishowen, Joseph O'Connor, éd. Secker & Warburg

Angela's Ashes, Frank McCourt, éd. Touchstone Books

TRIPS

Écosse, Philip Plisson & Patrick Mahé, Éditions du Chêne

Lighthouses, Philip Plisson & Guillaume Plisson, Watson Guptill Publications

Deux vagabonds en Irlande, Pierre Josse, Bertrand Pouchèle, éd. Terre de brume

Discover Islands of Ireland, Alex Ritsema, éd. Collins Press

Ionad Arann, les îles d'Aran, éd. Aran's Heritage Center.

Irlande de style géorgien, Herbert Ypma, éd. Assouline

L'Irlande ou les musiques de l'âme, under the direction of Pierre Joannon, éd. Artus

L'Irlande, Pat Coogan, éd. Romain Pagès

Tendre et fougueuse Irlande, Jill & Léon Uris, éd. Robert Laffont

HISTORY

Irlande, terre des Celtes, Pierre Joannon, Seamus Daly, éd. Ouest-France

Barry's Flying Column, éd. Ewan Butler

Wolfe Tone & the French Invasion of 1796, éd. Bantry Publications

Saint Patrick, Patrick Mey, éd. Coop Breizh

The Life Prayers of St Patrick, New York, Saint Patrick's Cathedral

The Road to Freedom, éd. Ard Mhusaem Na H Eireann

King Arthur, éd. Pitkin

Where They Lived in Dublin, John Cowell, éd. O'Brien Press

Le Chien du forgeron, Alain Deniel, éd. Picollec

Irish People, Kenneth Neill, éd. Gill & McMillan

GUIDES

Ireland, éd. Aer Lingus

Irlande, éd. Gallimard

Irlande, Collection « Voir » éd. Hachette

Irlande, le Guide du Routard, éd. Hachette

Une semaine en Irlande, collection Marco Polo, éd. Hachette

CHRONICLES

Connemara, Gilles Servat and Didier Houeix, éd. Apogée

Journal d'Irlande, Hervé Jaouen, éd. Ouest France

Chronique irlandaise, Hervé Jaouen, éd. Ouest France

Irlande, les Latins du Nord, under the direction of Michel Sailhan, éd. Autrement

WHISKEY

La Magie du whisky, Patrick Mahé and David Lefranc, Éditions du Chêne

Irish Pubs, éd. Real Ireland

MUSIC

Musique des mondes celtes, Jean-Pierre Pichard and Philip Plisson, Éditions du Chêne

Riverdance, éd. Media Pack

La musique celtique, Didier Convenant, éd. Hors Collection

The Dubliners, éd. Song book

MAPS

Historical Map of Ireland, L.G. Bullock, éd. Bartholomew

MAGAZINES

Neptunia, n° 30, éd. Musée de la marine

L'interceltique, Lorient

Armen

The Irish Eyes

Celtics

Finn McCool News

Les Nouvelles d'Irlande

FILMS

The Quiet Man (1952) by John Ford

Man of Aran (1934) by Robert Flaherty

Ryan's Daughter (1970) by David Lean

The Commitments (1991) by Alan Parker

The Snapper (1993) by Stephen Frears

Down the Corner (1977) de Joe Comerford

The Ballroom of Romance (1982) by Pat O'Connor

Maeve (1981) by Pat Murphy

Life After Life (1994) by Tim Fywell

The Secret of Roan Inish (1994) by John Sayles

Michael Collins (1996) by Neil Jordan

Acknowledgements

Martine "chachou" O'Douin
Chantal Piéton, Annie Pieussergues,
Jacques-Henry Bezy (Jameson, Dublin)
Mick "Warrior" Gerriet-Mahé

When I leave Ireland, whether it be day or night, and look back on the coast
disappearing on the horizon, I already know that I'll be back! I can't get over
Ireland. The Emerald Isle had obsessed me long before I had observed
it through my lenses. It was in the 70's when Marie and I had landed for the first time
at Wexford; it was our first trip out of the country. What a shock! For the first time
we were confronted with the impossibility of communicating, trying to understand
the incomprehensible. We are both children of the post-war. We were brought up on
the banks of the Loire River in France, where learning Shakespeare's language, was,
in the eyes of our families, our teachers, and our institutions, unnecessary. Our history
books had taught us that we had won the war, but never emphasized the origin of our friends
who had come to die on our beaches one morning in spring. The images of the Liberation
showed us that in Normandy as in Paris, the English speaking troops had probably
communicated without any difficulty.
Even if I have tried as well as possible, since this first experience, to get over this complex,
my level still doesn't permit me to share the depth of feeling that I would like to express
in words to say thank you to my Anglophone friends. My images are the expression of
the heart. I love Ireland and the Irish who have, in my eyes, a Latin soul.

Photographically yours,

Thank you to:
Brittany Ferries and its crews who have regularly transported us between Roscoff and Cork.
Météo-France and its marine weather prediction team, who have from Toulouse, guided us
daily about the winds. David Bedlow, of Irish Lighthouse who has done everything
for us to have exceptional contact with the staff and the keepers of the lighthouses.
Jacques Henri-Bezi, Colin Kavanagh and Leigh Ann Murphy of Irish Distillers who have
helped us understand whiskey culture.
Eric Oger of Atlantic Helicopters, our gentleman-pilot, who flew us from Nantes all around
the Irish coast. Christophe Le Potier, my assistant, who was very happy to organize on site
the production of these images, to drive the van, steer the boat, to change the film cartridges,
to develop the film, to prepare breakfast, etc…Jean-Marie Guillois and his sister
Marianne who invited us to Mont Juliet's High Mass.
Michael Hennessy, the Irish Helicopter pilot who dropped us off on another world in all
kinds of weather.

www.plisson.com – email: philip@plisson.com

*17th of January, 1998, morning of heavy weather on the Mullet Peninsula in
Mayo County. This 500th of a second shot of Christophe Le Potier, my assistant,
illustrates the 500th of a second shot that graces the cover of this book.*

The images have been made, as always,
with Canon EOS cartridges and lenses and Fuji film.

Translated into English by
Viviane Vagh and Jonathan Levine

Paste-up
Vu par…, Nantes

Binding
SMRF, Muzillac

Photoengraving
Le Govic, Nantes – France

Printing
Toppan Publishing Co., Hong Kong

First published in France in 2000 by Editions du Chêne-Hachette Livre.

This edition published by Barnes & Noble, Inc., by arrangement
with Editions du Chêne-Hachette Livre.

2002 Barnes & Noble Books
M 10 9 8 7 6 5 4 3 2 1
ISBN 0-7607-3057-1